ABC's on the Ranch

AuthorHouse™
1663 Liberty Drive
Bloomington, IN 47403
www.authorhouse.com
Phone: 1 (800) 839-8640

Published by AuthorHouse 01/09/2017

ISBN: 978-1-5246-5092-6 (sc)
978-1-5246-5093-3 (e)
978-1-5246-5541-9 (h)

Library of Congress Control Number: 2016919639

Print information available on the last page.

Any people depicted in stock imagery provided by Thinkstock are models,
and such images are being used for illustrative purposes only.
Certain stock imagery © Thinkstock.

This book is printed on acid-free paper.

authorHOUSE®

ABC's on the Ranch

Written by Michelle Provost

All photography was taken by Michelle Provost with the exception of Ann Burkholder (alfalfa field and swather), Gwen Shepperson (dog), Naomi Loomis (jingle bob spurs) Terryn Drieling (cover, calves, and windmill), and Jesse Mae Dalton (yearling).

Special thanks to Terryn Drieling, Elaine Peters, Destiny Killpack, my husband, and children.

IS FOR ALFALFA

IS FOR **BARN**

C

IS FOR CALVES

faith family and beef

D

IS FOR DOG

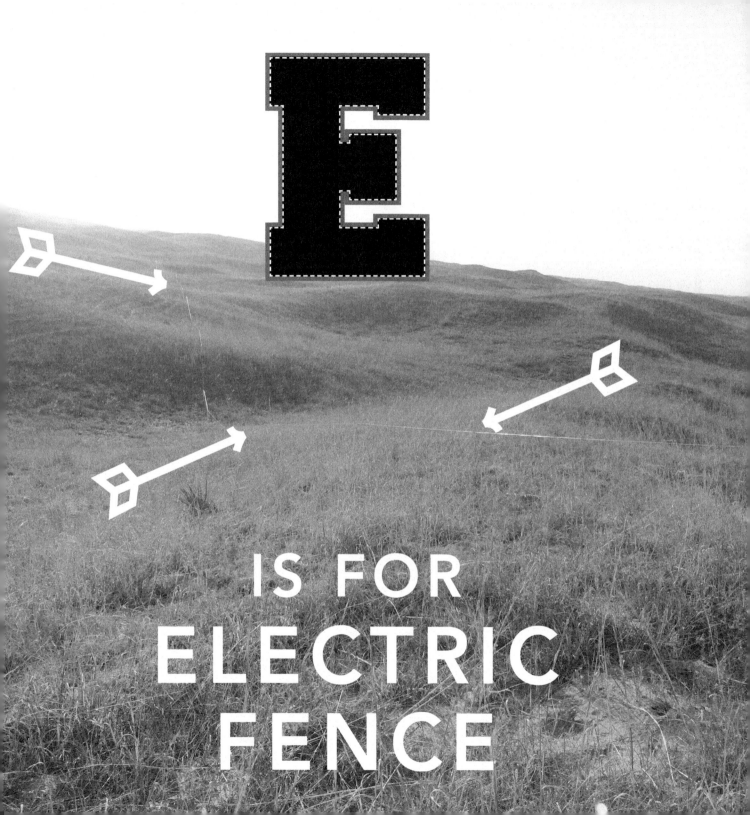

E

IS FOR
ELECTRIC
FENCE

IS FOR
FIXING FENCE

G IS FOR GATE

H

IS FOR **HORSES**

IS FOR BRANDING IRON

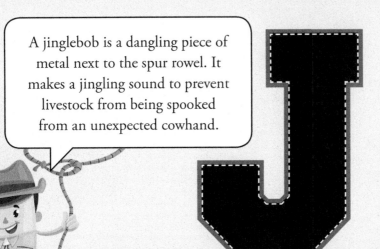

A jinglebob is a dangling piece of metal next to the spur rowel. It makes a jingling sound to prevent livestock from being spooked from an unexpected cowhand.

J IS FOR

JINGLE BOB SPURS

K IS FOR **KITTEN**

L

IS FOR LASSO

Beef cattle need minerals to be productive and healthy.

IS FOR MINERAL

IS FOR NEIGHBORS

IS FOR
OPEN RANGE

P

IS FOR
PUPPIES

A quirt is a short-handled riding whip with a braided leather lash.

IS FOR QUIRT

IS FOR ROUNDUP

IS FOR SADDLE

T

IS FOR TRAILER

IS FOR **UDDER**

IS FOR VACCINE

IS FOR **WINDMILL**

Ranching is a family business. Kids learn by example at an early age.

IS FOR EXAMPLE

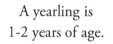

A yearling is
1-2 years of age.

IS FOR
YEARLING

These chaps, held
together with a zipper,
protect a cowboy
or cowgirl's legs.

IS FOR ZIPPER

About the Author

Michelle and her family enjoy pushing cows across a beautiful Nebraska ranch. As a native of Star Valley, Wyoming, she is at home in the saddle and wide open spaces. A passionate educator, she has taught students for more than 15 years in a variety of venues, including public schools, home school, and online. This is her first children's book. When she's not on the tractor or riding the range she plans to continue writing more children's books. Look for more upcoming titles in her ABC series.

CPSIA information can be obtained
at www.ICGtesting.com
Printed in the USA
LVOW06s0002290817
546737LV00020B/234/P